Fortune-Telling
WITH
PLAYING CARDS

by P.R.S. Foli

[1915]

First published in 2013 by Creole Moon Publications

This edition Copyright © 2013 Denise Alvarado

ISBN-10: 1490549048 (paper)
EAN-13: 978-1490549040 (paper)

Primary Category: Reference/Handbooks & Manuals
Country of Publication: United States
Publication Date: 15 day of the 3rd Moon, 2013
Language: English

Library of Congress Cataloging-in-Publication Data pending

Cover design by Denise Alvarado
Cover Image is in the Public Domain
Interior by Denise Alvarado
Interior Images are in the Public Domain

TABLE OF CONTENTS

Fortune-Telling
WITH
PLAYING CARDS

SIGNIFICATIONS OF THE CARDS USING A FULL DECK OF 52 CARDS.

The following definitions are based upon one of the oldest authorities dealing with the subject, and have been amplified by some of the more modern meanings now in vogue.

HEARTS

Ace. An important card, whose meaning is affected by its environment. Among hearts it implies love, friendship, and affection; with diamonds, money and news of distant friends; with clubs, festivities, and social or domestic rejoicing; with, spades, disagreements, misunderstandings, contention, or misfortune; individually, it stands for the house.

King. A good-hearted man, with strong affections, emotional, and given to rash judgments, possessing more zeal than discretion.

Queen. A fair woman, loving and lovable, domesticated, prudent, and faithful.

Knave. Not endowed with any sex. Sometimes taken as Cupid; also as the best friend of the inquirer, or as a fair person's thoughts. The cards on either side of the knave are indicative of the good or bad nature of its intentions.

Ten. A sign of good fortune. It implies a good heart, happiness, and the prospect of a large family. It counteracts bad cards and confirms good ones in its vicinity.

Nine. The wish card. It is the sign of riches, and of high social position accompanied by influence and esteem. It may be affected by the neighborhood of bad cards.

Eight. The pleasures of the table, convivial society. Another meaning implies love and marriage.

Seven. A faithless, inconstant friend who may prove an enemy.

Six. A confiding nature, liberal, open-handed,

HEART

and an easy prey for swindlers; courtship, and a possible proposal.

Five. Causeless jealousy in a person of weak, unsettled character.

Four. One who has remained single till middle life from being too hard to please.

Three. A warning card as to the possible results of the inquirer's own want of prudence and tact.

Deuce. Prosperity and success in a measure dependent on the surrounding cards; endearments and wedding bells.

DIAMONDS.

Ace. A ring or paper money.

King. A fair man, with violent temper, and a vindictive, obstinate turn of mind.

Queen. A fair woman, given to flirtation, fond of society and admiration.

Knave. A near relative who puts his own interests first, is self-opinionated, easily offended, and not always quite straight. It may mean a fair person's thoughts.

Ten. Plenty of money, a husband or wife from the country, and several children.

Nine. This card is influenced by the one accompanying it; if the latter be a court card, the person referred to will have his capacities discounted by a restless, wandering disposition. It may imply a surprise connected with money, or if in conjunction with the eight of spades it signifies cross swords.

Eight. A marriage late in life, which will probably be somewhat chequered.

Seven. This card has various meanings. It enjoins the need for careful action. It may imply a decrease of prosperity. Another reading connects it with uncharitable tongues.

Six. An early marriage and speedy widowhood. A warning with regard to second marriage is also included.

Five. To young married people this portends good children. In a general way it means unexpected news, or success in business enterprises.

Four. Breach of confidence. Troubles caused by inconstant friends, vexations and disagreeables.

Three. Legal and domestic quarrels, and probable un-Sappiness caused by wife's or husband's temper.

Deuce. An unsatisfactory love affair, awakening opposition from relatives or friends.

CLUBS.

Ace. Wealth, a peaceful home, industry, and general prosperity.

King. A dark man of upright, high-minded nature. calculated to make an excellent husband, faithful and true in his affections.

Queen. A dark woman, with a trustful, affectionate disposition, with great charm for the opposite sex, and susceptible to male attractions.

Knave. A generous, trusty friend, who will take trouble on behalf of the inquirer. It may also mean a dark man's thoughts.

Ten. Riches suddenly acquired, probably through the death of a relation or friend.

Nine. Friction through opposition to the wishes of friends.

Eight. Love of money, and a passion for speculating.

Seven. Great happiness and good fortune. If

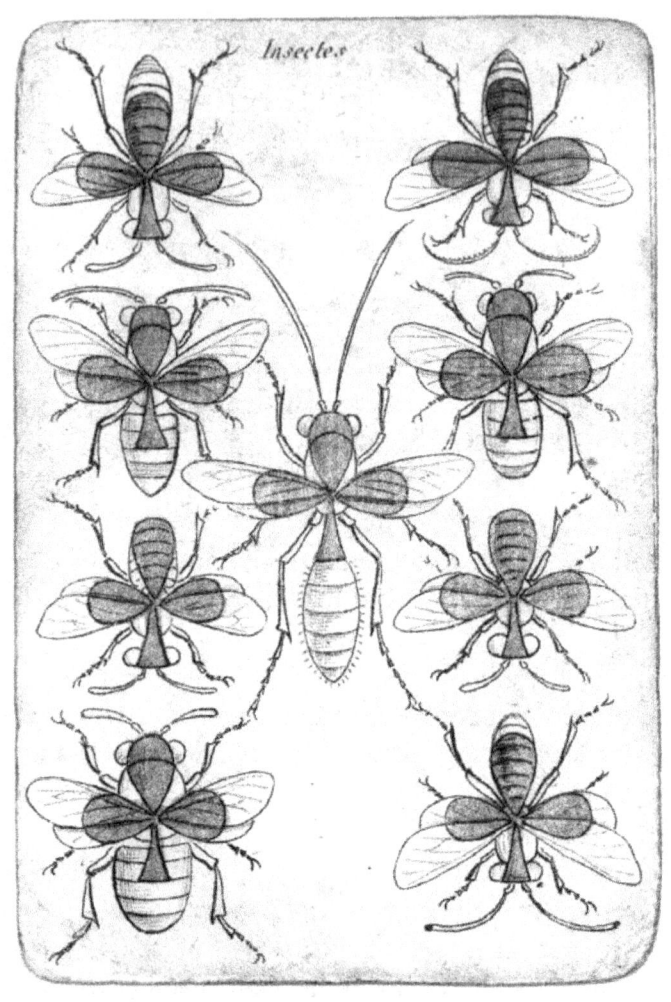

troubles come they will be caused by one of the opposite sex to the inquirer.

Six. Success in business both for self and children.

Five. An advantageous marriage.

Four. A warning against falsehood and double-dealing.

Three. Two or possibly three marriages, with money.

Deuce. Care is needed to avert disappointment, and to avoid opposition.

SPADES.

Ace. It may concern love affairs, or convey a warning that troubles await the inquirer through bad speculations or ill-chosen friends.

King. A dark man. Ambitious and successful in the higher walks of life.

Queen. A widow, of malicious and unscrupulous nature, fond of scandal and open to bribes.

Knave. A well-meaning, inert person, unready in action though kindly in thought.

Ten. An evil omen; grief or imprisonment. Has power to detract from the good signified by cards near it.

Nine. An ill-fated card, meaning sickness, losses, troubles, and family dissensions.

Eight. A warning with regard to any enterprise in hand, This card close to the inquirer means evil; also opposition from friends.

Seven. Sorrow caused by the loss of a dear friend.

Six. Hard work brings wealth and rest after toil.

Five. Bad temper and a tendency to interfere in the inquirer, but happiness to be found in the chosen wife or husband.

Four. Illness and the need for great attention to business.

Three. A marriage that will be marred by the inconstancy of the inquirer's wife or husband; or a journey.

Deuce. A removal, or possibly death.

ELEMENT.

L'EAU

NEPTUNE.

MYSTIC
MEANINGS.

There is fascination in certain calculations, and the following figures are not without a deep interest to those attracted by the study of Cartomancy.

- The fifty-two cards in the pack correspond with the fifty-two weeks in the year.

- The thirteen cards in each suit symbolise the thirteen lunar months, and the thirteen weeks in each quarter.

- There are four suits, as there are four seasons in the year. There are twelve court cards in the pack, just as there are twelve calendar months and twelve signs of the Zodiac.

SIGNIFICATIONS OF THE CARDS USING A FULL DECK OF 32 CARDS

Reduced Pack Generally Used.

 THE practice of using only thirty-two cards in telling fortune is very general, especially in those systems which have been adopted from or based upon a foreign source. We here give the definitions used in these methods, as they differ in certain respects from those given with the entire pack of fifty-two cards. Special care must be taken when using the selected pack to notice which way the cards come out upon the table, whether upright or reversed, as the meanings of the two positions may be diametrically opposed. (Editor's note: the 32 card deck consists of the Ace, King, Queen, Knave,

Ten, Nine, Eight, and Seven for each suit.)

HOW TO INDICATE REVERSED CARDS.

In former days it was easier to distinguish between the top and the bottom of a card, but now that they are practically made reversible, with a few exceptions, it is necessary to mark the cards that are to be used for fortune-telling in such a way as to enable the dealer to say at a glance whether the card is reversed or not. These marks should be made before the pack has been used, and need not be altered if the cards are kept solely for this purpose. In the following pages this selected pack is required for several methods, and in the case of the Master Method it is augmented by the four twos taken from the excluded cards.

MEANING OF THE HEARTS.

Ace. A love letter, good news; reversed, a removal or a visit from a friend.

King. Fair man of generous disposition; reversed, a disappointing person.

Queen. Fair, good-natured woman; reversed,

she has had an unhappy love affair.

Knave. A young bachelor devoted to enjoyment; reversed, a military lover with a grievance.

Ten. Antidote to bad cards; happiness and success; reversed, passing worries.

Nine. The wish card, good luck; reversed, short sorrow.

Eight. Thoughts of marriage, affections of a fair person; reversed, unresponsiveness.

Seven. Calm content; reversed, boredom, satiety.

MEANING OF THE DIAMONDS.

Ace. A letter, an offer of marriage; reversed, evil tidings.

King. A very fair or white-haired man, a soldier by profession, and of a deceitful turn of mind; reversed, a treacherous schemer.

Queen. A fair woman, given to gossip and wanting in refinement; reversed, rather a spiteful flirt.

Knave. Subordinate official, who is untrust-worthy; reversed, a mischief-maker.
Ten. Travelling or a removal; reversed, ill-luck will attend the step.

Nine. Vexation, hindrances; reversed, domestic wrangling, or disagreement between lovers.

Eight. Love passages; reversed, blighted affec-tions.

Seven. Unkindly chat cynicism; reversed, stu-pid and unfounded slander.

MEANING OF THE CLUBS.

Ace. Good luck, letters or papers relating to money, pleasant tidings; reversed, short-lived happiness, a tiresome correspondence.

King. A dark man, warm-hearted and true as a friend, straight in his dealings; reversed, good intentions frustrated.

Queen. A dark woman, loving but hasty, and bearing no malice; reversed, harassed by jeal-ousy.

Knave. A ready-witted young man, clever at

his work and ardent in his love; reversed, irresponsible and fickle.

Ten. Prosperity and luxury; reversed, a sea voyage.

Nine. An unlooked-for inheritance, money acquired under a will; reversed, a small, friendly gift.

Eight. Love of a dark man or woman which, if accepted and reciprocated, will bring joy and well-being; reversed, an unworthy affection calculated to cause trouble.

Seven. Trifling financial matters; reversed, money troubles.

MEANING OF THE SPADES.

Ace. Emotional enjoyment; reversed, news of a death, sorrow.

King. A widower, an unscrupulous lawyer, impossible as a friend and dangerous as an enemy; reversed, the desire to work evil without the power.

Queen. Widow, a very dark woman; reversed, an intriguing, spiteful woman.

Knave. Legal or medical student, wanting in refinement of mind and manners; reversed, a treacherous character, fond of underhand measures.

Ten. Grief, loss of freedom; reversed, passing trouble or illness.

Nine. A bad omen, news of failure or death; reversed, loss of one near and dear by death.

Eight. Coming illness; reversed, an engagement cancelled or a rejected proposal, dissipation.

Seven. Everyday worries, or a resolve taken; reversed, silly stratagems in love-making.

THE SIGNIFICATION OF QUARTETTES, TRIPLETS, AND PAIRS COMBINATIONS OF COURT CARDS.

Four Aces. When these fall together they imply danger, financial loss, separation from friends, love troubles, and, under some conditions, imprisonment. The evil is mitigated in proportion to the number of them that are reversed.

Three Aces. Passing troubles, relieved by good news, faithlessness of a lover and consequent sorrow. If reversed, they mean foolish excess.

Two Aces. These portend union; if hearts and clubs it will be for good, if diamonds and spades, for evil, probably the outcome of jealousy. If one or both be reversed, the object of the union will fail.

Four Kings. Honors, preferment, good appointments. Reversed, the good things will be of less value, but will arrive earlier.

Three Kings. Serious matters will be taken in hand with the best result, unless any of the three cards be reversed, when it will be doubtful.

Two Kings. Co-operation in business, upright conduct and prudent enterprises to be crowned with success. Each one reversed represents an obstacle. All three reversed spell utter failure.

Four Queens. A social gathering which may be spoilt by one or more being reversed.

Three Queens. Friendly visits. Reversed, scandal, gossip, and possibly bodily danger to the inquirer.

Two Queens. Petty confidences interchanged, secrets betrayed, a meeting between friends. When both are reversed there will be suffering for the inquirer resulting from his own acts. Only one reversed means rivalry.

Four Knaves. Roistering and noisy conviviality. Any of them reversed lessens the evil.

Three Knaves. Worries and vexations from acquaintances, slander calling the inquirer's honor in question. Reversed, it foretells a passage at arms with a social inferior.

Two Knaves. Loss of goods, malicious schemes. If both are reversed the trouble is imminent; if one only, it is near.

COMBINATIONS OF PLAIN CARDS.

Four Tens. Good fortune, wealth, success in whatever enterprise is in hand. The more there are reversed, the greater number of obstacles in the way.

Three Tens. Ruin brought about by litigation. When reversed the evil is decreased.

Two Tens. Unexpected luck, which may be connected with a change of occupation. If one be reversed it will come soon, within a few weeks possibly; if both are reversed, it is a long way off.

Four Nines. Accomplishment of unexpected events. The number that are reversed stand for the time to elapse before the fulfillment of the surprise.

Three Nines. Health, wealth, and happiness. Reversed, discussions and temporary financial difficulties caused by imprudence.

Two Nines. Prosperity and contentment, possibly accompanied by business matter, testamentary

21

documents, and possibly a change of residence. Reversed, small worries.

Four Eights. Mingled success and failure attending a journey or the taking up of a new position. Reversed, undisturbed stability.

Three Eights. Thoughts of love and marriage, new family ties, honourable intentions. Reversed, flirtation, dissipation and foolishness.

Two Eights. Frivolous pleasures, passing love fancies, an unlooked-for development. Reversed, paying the price of folly.

Four Sevens. Schemes and snares, intrigue prompted by evil passions, contention and opposition. Reversed, small scores off impotent enemies.

Three Sevens. Sadness from loss of friends, ill-health, remorse. Reversed, slight ailments or unpleasant reaction after great pleasure.

Two Sevens. Mutual love, an unexpected event Reversed, faithlessness, deceit or regret.

VARIOUS CARDS READ TOGETHER.

- The ten of diamonds next to the seven of spades means certain delay.

- The ten of diamonds with the eight of clubs

tells of a journey undertaken in the cause of love.

- The nine of diamonds with the eight of hearts foretells for certain a journey.

- The eight of diamonds with the eight of hearts means considerable undertakings; with the eight of spades there will be sickness; and with the eight of clubs there is deep and lasting love.

- The seven of diamonds with the queen of diamonds tells of a very serious quarrel; with the queen of clubs we may look for uncertainty; with the queen of hearts there will be good news.

- The ten of clubs followed by an ace means a large sum of money; should these two cards be followed by an eight and a king, an offer of marriage is to be expected.

- When the nine, ace, and ten of diamonds fall together we may look for important news from a distance; and if a court card comes out after them a journey will become necessary.

- The eight and seven of diamonds in conjunction imply the existence of gossip and chatter to be traced to the inquirer.

- When the king, queen, knave, and ace of

one colour appearing in sequence it is a sign of marriage.

- Should the queen of spades and the knave of hearts be near, it shows there are obstacles in the way.

- The proximity of the eight of spades bodes ill to the couple in question, but their happiness will be assured by the presence of the eight of hearts and the eight of clubs.

- The ace of diamonds and the ten of hearts also foretell wedding bells.

- The seven of spades, with either a court card or the two of its own suit, betrays the existence of a false friend.

- The eight and five of spades coming together tell of jealousy that will find vent in malicious conduct.

- A number of small spades in sequence are significant of financial loss, possibly amounting to ruin.

- The king of hearts and the nine of hearts form a lucky combination for lovers.

- The nine of clubs joined to the nine of

hearts is indicative of affairs connected with a will likely to benefit the inquirer.

- The queen of spades is the sign of widowhood, but if accompanied by the knave of her own suit she is symbolical of a woman who is hostile and dangerous to the inquirer.

GENERAL MEANING OF THE SEVERAL SUITS.

- Hearts, as might well be supposed, are specially connected with the work of Cupid and Hymen. The suit has also close reference to affairs of the home and to both the domestic and social sides of life.

- Diamonds are mainly representative of financial matters. small and great, with a generally favourable signification.

- Clubs are the happiest omens of all. They stand for worldly prosperity, a happy home life with intelligent pleasures and successful undertakings.

- Spades, on the other hand, forebode evil. They speak of sickness, death, monetary losses and anxieties, separation from friends and dear ones, to say nothing of the minor worries of life. They are also representative of love, unaccompanied by reverence or respect, and appealing exclusively to the senses.

SOME LESSER POINTS TO NOTICE.

- When a number of court cards fall together it is a sign of hospitality, festive social intercourse, and gaiety of all kinds.

- Married people who seek to read the cards must represent their own life partner by the king or queen of the suit they have chosen for themselves, regardless of anything else. For example, a very dark man, the king of spades, must consider his wife represented by the queen of spades, even though she may be as fair as a lily and not yet a widow.

- Bachelors and spinsters may choose cards to personate their lovers and friends according to their coloring.

- Two red tens coming together foretell a wedding, and two red eights promise new garments to the inquirer.

26

- A court card placed between two cards of the same grade; for instance, two nines, two sevens, etc. shows that the one represented by that card is threatened by the clutches of the law, and may be lodged at His Majesty's expense.

- It is considered a good augury of success when, in dealing the cards out, those of lesser value than the knave are in the majority, especially if they are clubs.

- Should a military man consult the cards he must always be represented by the king of diamonds.

- It is always essential to cut cards with the left hand, there being a long-established idea that it is more intimately connected with the heart than the right.

- A round table is generally preferred by those who are in the habit of practising cartomancy.

- It is a matter of opinion as to whether the cards speak with the same clearness and accuracy when consulted by the inquirer without an intermediary.

- The services of an adept are generally supposed to be of great advantage, even when people have mastered the rudiments of cartomancy themselves.

- Patience, the power of putting two and two together, a quick intuitive perception, and a touch of mysticism in the character, are all useful factors in the pursuit of this pastime.

DIVINING THE PAST, PRESENT AND FUTURE.

THERE is a very simple and generally accepted method of studying the past, the present, and the future in the light of cartomancy. The selected pack of thirty-two cards is required, and they must be shuffled and cut in the ordinary way. After the cut the packs must not be placed one upon the other until the top card of the lower one and the bottom card of the upper one have been placed aside to form the surprise. The remaining thirty cards are then to be dealt into three equal packs which, beginning at the left, represent respectively the Past, the Present, and the Future.

We will suppose that the knave of hearts, a pleasure-seeking young bachelor, is the inquirer. The ten cards representing the Past are as follows:

The queen of clubs, reversed.
The king of diamonds, reversed.
The ten of clubs, reversed.
The nine of diamonds.
The eight of clubs.
The ace of diamonds, reversed.
The ace of hearts, reversed.
The knave of spades, reversed.
The queen of spades, reversed.
The eight of diamonds.

There are three pairs among the ten. Two queens, both reversed, which remind the inquirer that he has had to suffer from the consequences of his own actions. The two aces, also both reversed, refer to some partnership into which he entered with good intentions but which was doomed to failure. The two eights speak of his frivolous pleasures and countless evanescent love affairs.

WHAT THE CARDS SAY.

We will now see what the cards have to say, taken in order. We begin with the queen of clubs, reversed, a dark woman tormented by jealousy, in which she was encouraged by the king of diamonds, reversed, who is a treacherous schemer, wishing no good to the inquirer. The ten of clubs tells of a sea voyage, and is followed by the nine of diamonds, showing that there were vexations and annoyances on that voyage. The eight of clubs speaks of the Inquirer's having possessed the affections of a dark woman, who would have contributed largely to his prosperity and happiness. The ace of diamonds, reversed, represents evil tidings that reached him in connection with the ace of hearts, reversed, which stands for a change of abode, and emanating from the knave of spades, reversed, a legal agent who was not to be trusted. There was also the queen of spades, a designing widow, with whom he had, the eight of diamonds, certain love passages.

THE PRESENT.

The ten cards in the centre pack are as follows:

Ace of spades, reversed.
Seven of diamonds.
Eight of hearts.
Queen of hearts.
Seven of hearts.
Queen of diamonds, reversed.
Nine of spades.
King of hearts, reversed.
Knave of hearts, reversed.
Ten of diamonds.

In this pack we have only two pairs, two sevens speaking of mutual love; and two queens, one being reversed, which suggest rivalry. Taken in order the pack reads thus: The ace of spades, reversed, speaks of sorrow in which he will be treated with a certain amount of heartless chaff and want of sympathy, as it is followed by the seven of diamonds. The eight of hearts tells us that he is entertaining thoughts of marriage, with the queen of hearts, a fair, lovable girl; but the seven of hearts shows that he is very contented with his present condition and in no hurry to change it. He is amusing himself with the queen of diamonds, reversed, who is a born flirt, but more spiteful than he suspects, and who is next to the worst card in the pack, the nine of spades, indicative of the harm she does to him, and the failure of his matrimonial plans. He is cut out by the king of hearts, who thus causes him a serious disappointment, and we see him, himself, reversed as the lover with a grievance; the last card is the ten of diamonds, so he has decided to ease his heartache by travelling.

THE FUTURE.

This pack contains the following cards:

The knave of diamonds, reversed.

The seven of clubs.
The eight of spades, reversed.
The seven of spades, reversed.
The ten of spades.
The nine of hearts.
The king of clubs.
The ten of hearts.
The king of spades.
The ace of clubs, reversed.

The presence of four spades foretells that trouble awaits our bachelor. We again have a pair of sevens, but one is reversed, so he may expect deceit to be at work. The two tens promise him an unlooked-for stroke of tuck to be met with in a new walk in life, while the two kings speak of cooperation in business and of the success which will crown his upright and practical conduct. The wish card, the nine of hearts, and the ten of hearts in a great measure counteract the mischief represented by the spades. The inquirer must beware of the knave of diamonds, reversed, who is a mischief maker, who will make use of the seven of clubs, trifling financial matters, either to break off an engagement or to cause an offer of marriage to be refused, as shown by the eight of spades, reversed. The chagrined lover will have recourse to silly stratagems in his love-making, the seven of spades, reversed, and this error will cause him grief, even to the shedding of tears, the ten of spades. The wish card, the nine of hearts, however, brings him better luck in his love affairs through the instrumentality of his trusty, generous friend, the king of clubs. His ill-fortune is further discounted by the next card, the ten of hearts, which promises him prosperity and success. He will find an enemy in the king of spades, a dark widower, who is a lawyer by profession, and none too scrupulous in his ways. He may expect a good deal of troublesome correspondence with this man, as shown by the last card, the ace of clubs, reversed. The subject of this correspondence is possibly to be found in the surprise, which consists of the nine of clubs, reversed, meaning an unexpected acquisition of money under a will. He will do well to take heed when in the companionship of the knave of clubs, reversed, the second card of the surprise for he is a flatterer and a somewhat irresponsible character.

YOUR FORTUNE IN TWENTY-ONE CARDS

A reduced pack - An example - The three packs - The surprise.

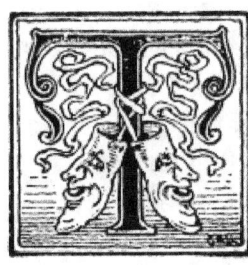 THIS method requires a pack of thirty-two cards, although only twenty-one of them are actually used in the process. The whole pack must be well shuffled and cut with the left hand. The dealer then takes off the first eleven cards and throws them aside. From the twenty-one left in his hand he takes the uppermost card and places it apart for "the surprise" before dealing out the other twenty and placing them in order on the table before him. If the card representing the inquirer is not among them the whole process must be repeated from the beginning.

The signification of the cards must be read, taking care to notice any set of two, three, or four of a kind, as their collective meaning should be added to the individual explanation.

After this has been done the twenty cards should be taken in order, starting from the left, and their meanings linked up together as a continuous message.

The cards must now be taken up again, shuffled, and cut as before. The dealer then makes them into three packs, having been careful to place the first card apart for "the surprise." Two of the packs will consist of seven cards, the third of only six. The inquirer is then asked to choose one of the packs, which must be exposed face upwards, moving from left to right, and these six or seven cards, as the case may be, should be read according to their significations. This operation is repeated three times, so that at the finish "the surprise" consists of three cards, which Are exposed and read last of all.

AN EXAMPLE.

The accompanying example will make the foregoing explanation more lucid and interesting.

We will take the knave of clubs as the representative of the inquirer, a dark, clever, well-intentioned young man. The twenty-one cards come out in the following order, beginning from the left:

The king of spades.
Queen of hearts, reversed.
Ace of hearts.
Knave of clubs.
Ace of spades, reversed.
Ace of clubs.
Knave of hearts.
King of hearts.
Queen of spades, reversed.
Nine of hearts.
Knave of diamonds.
Ten of spades.
Ace of diamonds, reversed.
King of diamonds.
Seven of diamonds.
Eight of diamonds.
Eight of spades, reversed.
Seven of clubs, reversed.
Nine of clubs, reversed.
Nine of diamonds.
The surprise, placed apart.

Before taking the individual significance of
each card we will look at some of the combinations. There are the four aces, telling of bad
news, relating to trouble through the affections, but two being reversed mitigate the evil,
and give a ray of hope to the inquirer. The
three kings tell of an important undertaking
which will be discussed and carried through

successfully by the young man, who has excellent abilities. The two queens, both reversed, warn the inquirer that he will suffer from the result of his own actions, more especially as the queen of spades in an inverted position represents a malicious and designing widow. It will be found as the process develops that she is very much to the fore with regard to the inquirer's affairs. The three knaves confirm the foregoing reading, for they betoken annoyances and worries from acquaintances, ending even in slander. The three nines, one of them reversed, speak of happiness and entire success in an undertaking, though the inversion shows that there will be a slight, passing difficulty to overcome. The two eights refer to flirtations on the part of the inquirer, and one being reversed warns him that he will have to pay for some of his fun. The two sevens tell of mutual love between the young man and the lady of his choice, but as the one is reversed there will be deceit at work to try and separate them.

Now let us see what the twenty cards have to say taken consecutively. We start off with the king of spades, a clever, ambitious, but unscrupulous man who has been instrumental in thwarting the love affairs of the fair, lovable, and tender-hearted woman, the queen of hearts, upon whom the inquirer has set his affections. The ace of hearts following her is the love letter she will receive from the inquirer, the knave of clubs; but he is next to the ace of spades, reversed, foretelling grief to him, which may affect his health, and the ace of clubs coming immediately after points to the cause being connected with money. The next three cards are court cards, and that means gaiety, in which the inquirer will be mixed up with a lively young bachelor - the knave of hearts - a fair, generous, but hot-tempered man - the king of diamonds - and the malicious, spiteful widow represented by the queen of spades, reversed. The inquirer will meet with pleasure, caused by success, the nine of hearts; but this is closely followed by the knave of diamonds, an unfaithful friend, who will try to bring disgrace, the ten of spades, upon his betters, and will write a letter containing unpleasant news - the ace of diamonds, reversed - which will concern or be prompted by the king of diamonds, a military man who has a grievance with regard to his love affairs and who is not above having recourse to scandal, the seven of diamonds, to avenge his wounded vanity. The next card is the eight of diamonds, the sign of some love-making, but our young people are not at the end of their troubles yet, for the eight of spades, reversed, tells us that his offer of marriage will be rejected. The seven of clubs is a card of caution, and implies danger from the opposite sea, so we gather that the spiteful widow has been at work, and is possibly to blame for his rejection; this idea is further strengthened by the nine of clubs, also reversed, coming immediately, which suggests letters that may have done the mischief. The nine of diamonds tells of the annoyance caused by these events, and their effect upon the affections of a dark person, the inquirer, who is a man well worth having.

THE THREE PACKS.

In the first deal the inquirer chooses the middle pack, which contains the following cards: the knave of diamonds, the seven of diamonds, the ace of clubs, the queen of spades, reversed, the ace of spades, the ace of diamonds, the eight of diamonds.

We notice that three aces come out in this pack and show passing troubles in love affairs. The knave of diamonds, an unfaithful friend, is mixed up in scandal, the seven of diamonds, conveyed in a letter, the ace of clubs, written or instigated by the spiteful widow, the queen of spades. The ace of spades betokens sickness, but it is followed by the ace of diamonds, the wedding ring, and the pack closes with the eight of diamonds, telling of a happy marriage for the inquirer after all his worries. In the second deal he again selects the middle pack, and we see the following: the queen of spades, reversed as usual, the nine of clubs, reversed, the seven of clubs, reversed, the nine of hearts, the seven of diamonds, the eight of clubs.

There are two nines, one reversed, speaking of small worries, and two sevens, one reversed, which show there is deceit at work. The pack reads thus: the queen of spades, the spiteful widow, who seems to be ubiquitous, is followed by the nine of clubs, representing the letter referred to above, and the seven of clubs standing next to it sounds a word of caution to the inquirer as to his lady friend, so-called; be will probably succeed in outwitting the widow, for the next card is the nine of hearts, implying joy and success in spite of scandal, the seven of diamonds with reference to his affections represented by the eight of clubs.

The Three Packs

	ONE CHOSEN BY THE INQUIRER	

What the first selected pack contains—

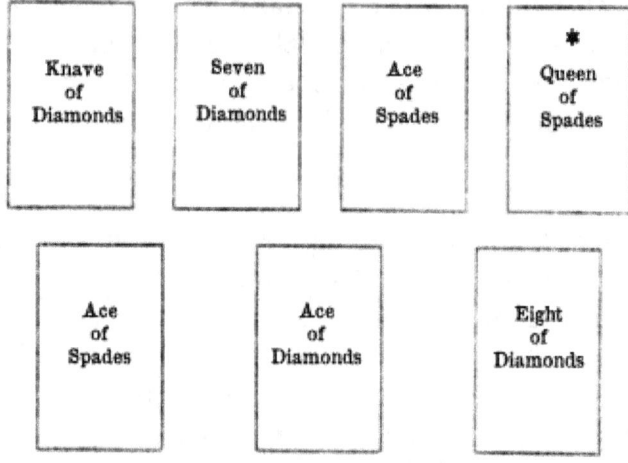

The three cards forming the Surprise—

* Means "reversed"

In the third deal, the inquirer still is faithful to the middle pack, and we find the following cards: the ace of diamonds, ten of spades, reversed, queen of spades, reversed, nine of diamonds, reversed, seven of clubs, reversed, ace of clubs, reversed. The two aces, one of them reversed, tell of a union between two parties, but as the colours cross and one is reversed the result will not be known at present. Here, we get the wedding-ring, the ace of diamonds, followed by the ten of spades, reversed, which speaks of brief sorrow, occasioned doubtless by the spiteful widow, who again appears reversed, and intent upon mischief; next to her comes the nine of diamonds, reversed, signifying a love quarrel; the seven of clubs, reversed, gives a word of caution to the inquirer with regard to the opposite sex; the last card is the ace of clubs, reversed, which means joy soon followed by sorrow.

It is remarkable that the queen of spades comes out in each of the packs and is reversed every time.

THE SURPRISE.

The surprise is now turned up and contains the king of spades, a dark, ambitious unscrupulous man who has interfered with the love affairs of the fair woman, the queen of hearts, to whom the inquirer has made an offer, so far without success; the third card is the nine of hearts, reversed, which tells that it will be but a passing cloud that will separate the lovers.

PROSPÉRITÉ

GENIE DE LA PAIX

44

THE 21 CARD METHOD
COMBINATION OF SEVENS

A method with selected cards - General rules - How to proceed - Reading of the cards - Signification of cards - Some combinations - A typical example - Further inquiries - The seven packs.

A METHOD WITH SELECTED CARDS.

 THIS method is very simple, and as it takes but a short time, is more suitable when there are many fortunes to read. A little practice will soon enable a would-be cartomancer to construe the various combinations, as there are so few cards to remember.

45

It may be objected that meanings are now given different from those taught in the first method. This is certainly a fact, but it also an advantage; one method may suit one person's abilities and intuitiveness better than another, and so enable a more comprehensive reading to be given from the diminished pack than from the full Tarot pack.

GENERAL RULES.

Thirty-two cards only are selected from an ordinary pack of playing cards. In each suit the ace, king, queen, knave, ten, nine, eight, and seven are retained; all the others, those from two to six inclusively, are discarded. The cards must be shuffled and cut into three sections by the inquirer, each cut being turned face upwards. The manipulator must carefully note the result of these cuts, as they give au indication of what is coming. Then the centre pack is to be takes first, the last neat, and the first last of all. Holding this newly arranged pack in the left hand, draw off three cards, and facing them upwards, select the highest card of any suit that may appear. Retain this one and put the others aside for the next deal. Proceed in this way until you have finished the pack, then shuffle all the discard together, and repeat until you have any number over twenty-one on the table. If three cards of any suit should appear, or three cards of the same value, they are all to be taken. It must not be forgotten that the cards are also selected from the "cuts," and should the lifting of one card reveal another of greater value of the same suit exposed, then that also is retained.

HOW TO PROCEED.

The first question to decide is which card will represent the inquirer. This is generally settled according to the complexion: diamonds for the very fair; hearts, those of medium colouring; clubs for brunettes with brown hair; and spades for those of dark complexion. This suit also represents elderly people. A king represents a man, and a queen a woman. This representative card is not to be drawn out; it is shuffled with the others, and taken when it is the highest of its suit. The only exception to this rule is, when there have been already twenty-one or more cards selected, then it must be taken from the remainder and placed last of all.

READING OF THE CARDS.

The reading in this method is from left to right, and the cards are to be placed in a semicircle or horse-shoe, in the order they are drawn. Court cards represent people, and the numbers relate to events. Generally diamonds relate to money and interest; hearts, to the affections; clubs, to business; spades, to the more serious affairs of life. The signification of each card is given separately, as well as of some of the combinations, and an example of a fortune is worked out, the study of which will more easily enable a student to understand this method.

SIGNIFICATION OF CARDS.

HEARTS
King. A man with brown hair and blue eyes.
Queen. A woman with similar complexion.
Knave. A friend with good intentions.
Ten. Marriage.
Nine. Wish.
Eight. Affection.
Seven. Friendship.
Ace. House.

DIAMONDS
King. A fair man.
Queen. A fair woman.
Knave. A friend.
Ten. Wealthy marriage.

Nine. Rise in social position.
Eight. Success with speculation.
Seven. A good income.
Ace. A wedding or present of jewelry.

CLUBS

King. A man who is neither fair nor dark.
Queen. A woman in middle life.
Knave. A business friend.
Ten. Journey by water.
Nine. Successful business.
Eight. Pleasure in society.
Seven. A business affair.
Ace. A letter, check, or legal document.

SPADES

King. A dark man.
Queen. A dark woman or widow.
Knave. Personal thoughts.
Ten. Journey by land.
Nine. Illness or sorrow.
Eight. Loss.
Seven. A disagreement.
Ace (right way). Responsible position in the service of the crown.
Ace (upside down). Sorrow or death.

SOME OF THE COMBINATIONS.

Three kings: a new friend; two kings and a knave: meeting with an old friend; three knaves: legal business; three queens: a disagreement with women; three tens, very fortunate combination. If the ten of clubs and the ten of hearts appear with the ten of diamonds, it will easily be seen that a wealthy marriage will take place after a journey across the water.

Three nines: very speedy good news; three eights: a removal; three sevens: speedy news, but not altogether satisfactory; three aces: very good fortune; the ace of clubs and the ace of diamonds would signify an offer of marriage by letter.

The ace and nine of hearts mean that you will have the realization of your heart's desire in your own house; the ace and nine of spades: that sorrow and death will come to your family; the king and queen of any suit, with the ten of hearts, Is a sign that you will hear of a marriage shortly.

A TYPICAL EXAMPLE.

Now we will proceed to read a fortune, and

for the subject we will take the queen of hearts. The first shuffle and division of the pack into three reveals three hearts - king, knave, and seven - which indicates that the lady whom the queen represents has a firm man friend, who is neither fair nor dark. These three cards are taken and laid in order, beginning on the left hand.

Then the packs having been taken in order as described, and held in the left hand, the fortune-teller proceeds to draw off three cards, and make his selection according to the rule. The pack being finished, the process is repeated twice more.

In three deals the fortune of the queen of hearts revealed the following cards, and if a student will take a pack of cards and select the same, he can judge how the various combinations may be read.

King, knave, seven of hearts, ace of clubs, king of spades, queen of clubs, queen of diamonds, queen of spades, king of clubs, knave of diamonds, ace of hearts, knave of spades, king of diamonds, knave of clubs, queen of hearts, ace of diamonds, ten of hearts, eight of clubs, seven of spades, ace of spades, ten of clubs, ten of spades, ten of diamonds. Now, from the queen of hearts we will proceed to count seven, taking into consideration the way the lady's face is turned. It is to the left, consequently the seventh card from her is the queen of spades, the seventh from which is the king of hearts, and the seventh again is the ten of hearts. I read this that the lady has some good friends; but that the woman whom the queen of spades represents will resent her marriage, but without effect. The next card is the knave of diamonds, followed by the seven of hearts and the seven of spades—a combination which represents some speedy news, not exactly to the advantage of the inquirer. The knave of spades, followed by the king and the ten of clubs, denotes that a dark man, who is separated from the queen of hearts, is constantly thinking of her and hoping for a speedy reunion.

The knave of clubs and the queen of diamonds come next. Knaves and women form a conjunction that never brings good luck; but in this case they are followed by the ten of diamonds, one of the most fortunate cards in the pack. The ace of diamonds and the king of clubs follow, which means an offer of marriage shortly. The queen of hearts is indeed a sad coquette, for there is no indication that she accepts this, as the knave of hearts, with the eight of clubs and the ace of hearts, are quickly on the scene. It appears that there is another wooer who comes to her home and is received with pleasure.

More serious affairs appear now; the ace of clubs, with the ace of spades and the king of diamonds, signify that the lady is likely to have some business with which a woman darker than herself is connected. This will lead to a considerable journey, which she will immediately take, as the card denoting this counts seven directly to her.

Now we will look at the cards as they lie on the table. For a reading taken at random they foretell a very good future. All the court cards and the aces and tens are out, with the seven of hearts and the eight of clubs, and all are cards of favorable import.

Three queens together generally betoken some mischief or scandal, but as they are guarded by kings it will probably not amount to much. The ace of diamonds and the ten of hearts placed so near the representative card would surely tell us of a forthcoming marriage, except that the queen has her face turned away from it. The three tens placed as they are tell of prosperity after journeys by land and water. Now we will pair the cards and see if any more meaning can be extracted from them. On land and on the water this lady will meet a rich man who will entertain a strong affection for her. I must not omit to mention that the cards are paired from the extreme ends of the horse-shoe. Thus the king of hearts and the ten of diamonds, knave of hearts and ten of spades, &c. The business appears again, and a dark man seems to be in some perplexity. The three queens are not yet separated and are in closer connection with the inquirer than ever. Oh! there will be chatting over the tea-cups about a marriage. The fair damsel herself appears to be a little more inclined to matrimony, but the three knaves imply that she will have some difficulty in settling her affairs. The two kings imply that she has some staunch friends, and that the result will be quite satisfactory. A general reading gives the impression that the queen of hearts is of a lovable disposition and fond of society, as so many court cards came out, and if the three queens meant a little gossip it was in a kindly spirit.

FURTHER INQUIRIES.

There is another little ceremony to be gone through which will tell us if she is likely to have her "heart's desire" realized. The nine of hearts, which is the symbol of a wish, did not appear, so that she is apparently very cool and neutral. However, the other cards may tell us something.

The used cards are to be shuffled and cut once by the inquirer, and she may wish for anything she likes during the process. Then the cards are laid out one at a time in seven packs - six packs in a semicircle, and one in the centre - the cards of the last are to be turned face upwards, but none of the other cards are to be exposed until the end.

THE SEVEN PACKS.

The seven packs represent respectively - "yourself," "your house," "what you expect," "what you don't expect," "a great surprise," "what is sure to come true," and "the wish." The cards, having been shuffled and cut once, are dealt out in the manner described, and these are the combinations we get:

First Pack. Queen of spades, queen of hearts, ten of clubs, seven of hearts.
Second. Ace of spades, knave of clubs, ace of diamonds, and ten of spades.
Third. Knave of spades, king of diamonds, knave of hearts.
Fourth. Queen of clubs, seven of spades, king of spades.
Fifth. Ten of diamonds, eight of clubs, and queen of diamonds.

Sixth. King of hearts, ten of hearts, king of clubs. Wish. Ace of hearts, knave of diamonds, ace of clubs.

The first pack represents to me the meeting of the inquirer with a dark or elderly woman, for whom she has a strong affection. Water is crossed before that meeting takes place. The second pack reads as if a dark man would offer a ring or a present of jewelry, and also that he is meditating a journey by land. He is probably a professional man, or in the service of the Crown.

The third pack, with its combination of knaves and king, has reference to business transactions which will most probably be favorable to the interests of the queen.

The fourth pack presages some slight disappointment, illness, or unhappiness in connection with some friends.

The fifth pack tells us that same brilliant fortune is awaiting a fair friend that will lead to a higher social position.

The sixth pack tells us that, perhaps, our seemingly indifferent queen of hearts has a slight tenderness for some one. He is older than she is, and is only waiting for an opportunity to declare his affection. If the wish related to such a man as I have described, she may be certain of its fulfillment, even should there be a slight delay.

The seventh or wish pack is extremely good, and tells us that many affairs will be transacted by writing.

The future of the queen of hearts is fair and bright, her disposition is lovable, and she will bring happiness to other people.

This example is not made up of selected cards. They were shuffled, cut, and drawn in the ordinary way. I say this because so few cards of bad import have appeared, and it might be thought these were chosen in order to avoid prophesying disappointments.

In the foregoing example twenty-three cards were dealt out, but the number may vary. It must, however, be an uneven number. Sometimes only fifteen or seventeen cards are taken, and with the smaller quantity of selected cards there is an optional way of concluding operations. After having read the pairs, the cards are gathered up, shuffled, and cut into three packs instead of seven. These three are placed in a row, and a fourth card is put apart for the surprise. The inquirer is requested to choose one of the three packs, which represent respectively For the house, For those who did not expect it, and For the inquirer - the last being decided by the choice of the person in question.

When these three packs have been duly read, all the cards are again taken up except The Surprise (which is left face downwards on the table), and dealt out again, the same process being repeated three times until there are three cards set aside for the surprise. These are read last of all, and form the concluding message to the inquirer. Let's hope it may be a cheerful one!

ANOTHER METHOD

General outline - Signification of cards - How to consult the cards - An illustration - Its reading.

HERE again the pack of thirty-two cards is used, the cards from two to six inclusively being discarded, as in "The Combination of Sevens."

GENERAL OUTLINE.

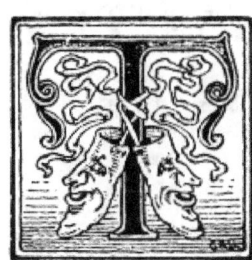 The general meaning pertaining to each suit is as follows: The court cards bear the signification of people, and the king, queen, and knave in each suit suggest relationship. The kings indicate the profession followed. Thus, the king of spades denotes a literary man, or one whose desires would lead him to the pulpit or the platform.

59

The king of hearts is the symbol of a wealthy man - one who deals with large sums of money - for instance, a banker, capitalist, or stockbroker.

The king of clubs indicates the mental side of business, and here we look for the lawyer or barrister.

The king of diamonds is a business man - one who will depend on both his brain and hands for work. Diamonds are eminently the practical suit, and must always be consulted with reference to the subject's condition in life. They signify the material side of life, and according to the needs, so this suit indicates success, or the absence of it - failure. There is a very slight variation in the signification of the cards as given in the preceding method, but it is well to observe it carefully, as the mode of procedure is entirely different.

SIGNIFICATION OF CARDS.

HEARTS
Ace. Quiet and domestic happiness
Seven. Love
Eight. A surprise
Nine. A wish
Ten. A wedding

SPADES
Ace. Service under the Crown
Reverse Ace. A death
Seven. Unpleasant news
Eight. Sorrow or vexation
Nine. Quarrels
Ten. A disappointment

DIAMONDS
Ace. A letter or ring
Seven. A journey
Eight. Society
Nine. Illness or sews of a birth
Ten. Money, joy, success

CLUBS
Ace. A present
Seven. Gain; good business
Eight. Pleasure
Nine. A proposal
Ten. A journey by Water

HOW TO CONSULT THE CARDS.

The inquirer is to shuffle the pack of cards and cut it into three. Take up the cards and let your subject draw any chance card that he pleases. Place this card on the table, and the suit from which it is drawn will determine the representative card, as it is an indication of the character of your subject.

A lady is represented by a queen, a man by a king, and the knave stands for the male relations or thoughts.

After the card is drawn, place the remainder on the table in four rows, beginning each row from left to right.

The cards that immediately surround the king or queen aid us in our judgment of the inquirer; and remember that the right hand card is the more important one.

AN ILLUSTRATION.

A practical illustration will exemplify my meaning, and again we will suppose a lady has cut the cards to have her fortune read. The cards being shuffled and cut into three, the card was drawn, and as this proved to be a seven of clubs, so the queen represented the subject in this instance. When the cards were placed in order this is how they appeared.

First line. Seven of clubs, eight of clubs, king of clubs, seven of hearts, king of diamonds, nine of diamonds, ten of diamonds, king of hearts.

Second line. Seven of spades, nine of spades, knave of hearts, king of spades, eight of spades, queen of spades, ten of spades, ace of diamonds.

Third line. Ace of spades, knave of clubs, queen of clubs, ten of hearts, ace of hearts, queen of diamonds, ace of clubs, nine of hearts.

Fourth line. Knave of spades, seven of diamonds, eight of hearts, nine of clubs, eight of diamonds, knave of diamonds, queen of hearts, ten of clubs.

ITS READING.

Now we can proceed with the reading: As the suit of clubs is a pleasant one, we may conclude the lady is of a cheerful temperament. The seven itself signifies gain and prosperity, and the eight pleasure, which come to the inquirer through the king of clubs - typical of a solicitor. The seven of hearts indicates that a fair man is in love with the inquirer. The nine of diamonds, with the joyful ten beside it, seems to foretell a birth, and the king of hearts stands for a good friend. But the seven and nine of spades, in conjunction, inform us that some annoyance is coming which is possibly connected with the king of hearts. The king of spades, accompanied by the eight of that suit, tells that this man is suffering considerable grief and vexation on account of the queen of clubs, suffering which will cause another woman to be jealous.

The queen and ten of spades, with the ace of spades, imply disagreeable tidings; but as the knave of clubs appears side by side with the queen of that suit (the inquirer), and they are followed by the ten of hearts, it will in no wise disturb the affection of either. The knave here may be taken to indicate the thoughts or intentions of the king. The ace of hearts seems to promise great tranquility and happiness in the domestic life. A near relation, one deeply interested in the queen of clubs, is represented by the queen of diamonds. The ace of clubs shows that a letter is on its way.

The nine of hearts, the wish or betrothal card, follows, and from this I should infer that a proposal of marriage will come by letter, and one which will most probably be accepted. The knave of spades is followed by the seven of diamonds and the eight of hearts, which shows that the queen of clubs has been much loved by some one, and that an offer of marriage will have to be considered either directly before or immediately after a journey. The inquirer will have a great deal of pleasure on a journey. The queen of hearts and knave of diamonds indicate good friends who show her much kindness, and there will be welcome tidings for her across the water.

Now, count the rows, and should the betrothal card (the nine of hearts) appear in the third or fourth row, that number of years must elapse before becoming affianced.

Count the rows again until the one in which the ten of hearts (the marriage card) appears. In this example the betrothal and marriage card both appear in the third row, which indicates that the inquirer will be engaged in about three years, and marriage will take place soon after.

A FRENCH METHOD

French system - The reading - An example.

FRENCH SYSTEM.

TAKE the pack of thirty-two cards, shuffle them thoroughly, then cut them in the usual way and deal them out in two packs of sixteen cards each. The inquirer must choose one of the packs and the first card is placed apart to supply the surprise. The remaining fifteen cards must then be turned face upwards, and placed in order, from left to right, before the dealer. It is essential that the card representing the inquirer should be found in the pack selected by him or her, otherwise it is useless to proceed; so the cards must be shuffled, cut, and dealt out over and over again, until the representative card is found in the right quarter.

THE READING.

The reading is conducted as follows. First, take any two, three, or four of a kind, kings, knaves, eights, or whatever may appear, and give their explanation as pairs, triplets, or quartettes; then start from the representative card, and count in sevens, moving from right to left; thirdly, pair the end cards together and consider their meaning. The next move is to shuffle the fifteen cards again, cut, and deal them out into three packs, each of which will naturally have five cards. The uppermost card of the three packs is removed, and placed with that which has been set apart for "The Surprise," and by this arrangement there will be four packs containing an equal number of cards

The inquirer must then be asked to choose one of these packs for himself or herself, after which the four cards are exposed on the table from left to right, and their individual and collective meanings are read. The left hand pack will be for "The House," the third pack is "For Those Who do not Expect It," and the fourth supplies "The Surprise."

AN EXAMPLE.

Here is an example of the way in which the packs may turn out. We will suppose that the inquirer is represented by the queen of clubs. Her choice falls on the middle pack, which contains the following cards: the knave of clubs, the eight of diamonds, reversed,, the eight of hearts, and the queen of spades.

1. FOR THE INQUIRER.

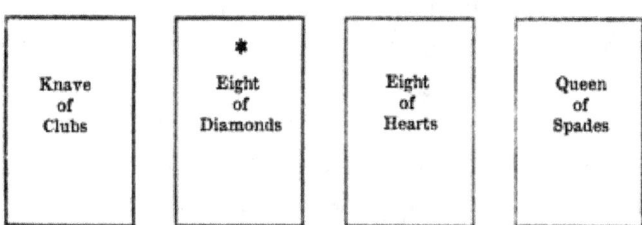

The reading will be thus, taking the cards in the above order;—The thoughts of the inquirer are running upon an unsuccessful love-affair, and, though moving in good society, she is exposed to the interference of a dark, malicious widow.

The next pack, standing for "The House," is made up of the knave of spades, the ace of spades, the king of spades, and the knave of hearts. We will take their signification as they stand. The three spades mean disappointment. The presence of two knaves together speaks of evil intentions.

The legal agent, knave of spades, is employed

in some underhand business by his master, king of spades, the dishonest lawyer, who is an enemy to the inquirer just as he is that of her friend, the festive, thoughtless young bachelor, knave of hearts, who follows him.

2. THE HOUSE.

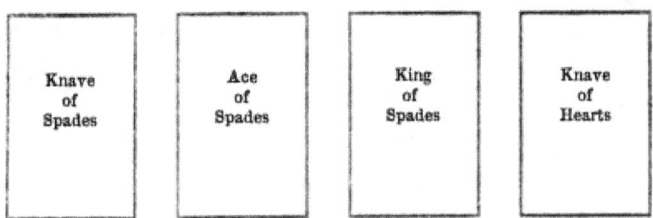

The third pack is composed of the nine of clubs, reversed, the ace of clubs, the ten of spades, and the queen of hearts. We find short-lived joy and good news, followed by tears, for the fair, soft-hearted lady, who is susceptible to the attractions of the other sex.

3. FOR THOSE WHO DO NOT EXPECT.

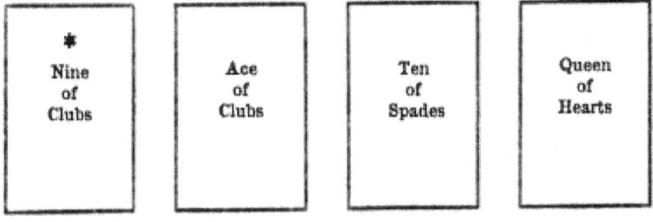

"The Surprise" is very closely connected with the inquirer herself, for we find her included in the four cards. There are the ace of hearts, the queen of clubs, the nine of diamonds, and the seven of diamonds. From this we gather that there is a love letter for the inquirer, which, however, may be delayed by some cross accident, and she will thus be exposed to the foolish ridicule of tactless, unkindly persons. But she will get the letter all the same.

4. THE SURPRISE.

Ace of Hearts	Queen of Clubs	Nine of Diamonds	Seven of Diamonds

THE GRAND STAR

The number of cards may vary - The method - The reading in pairs - Diagram of the Grand Star - An example.

THE NUMBER OF CARDS MAY VARY.

 THERE are various ways of telling fortunes with cards arranged in the form of a star, and whichever of these may be preferred, it will always be found necessary to use an uneven number of cards in addition to the one representing the inquirer. Some stars are done with thirteen cards, some with fifteen, and so on, but the real Grand Star must have twenty-one cards placed round the representative one.

THE METHOD.

Suppose the inquirer be a fair man, the king of hearts would be the card selected to form the centre of the star. This representative card

71

is placed face upwards on the table, and the remaining thirty-one cards of the pack (the twos, threes, fours, fives, and sixes having been previously removed) must then be shuffled, and cut with the left hand. In the accompanying diagram the cards are numbered in the order that they are placed in upon the table, taking the representative as No. 1. The mode of withdrawing the cards from the pack is as follows: The first ten cards are thrown aside after the first cut, and the eleventh card is placed below No. 1; then cut out a second time, and place the top card of the pack on the table above No. 1; cut a third time, take the bottom card of the pack in the hand and place it to the left of No. s. The cards must be cut every time a card is to be withdrawn, and they are taken alternately from the top and bottom of the pack as above directed. Great care should be observed in the placing of the cards in due order, as any deviation will affect the reading at a subsequent stage of the process. The last card, No. 22, is placed across the foot of the representative.

THE READING IN PAIRS.

When the Grand Star has been thus formed, the cards must read in pairs, taking the outside circle in this order: 14 and 16, 21 and 19, 15 and 17, 20 and 18. Then take the inner circle, moving from left to right thus: 6 and 10, 9 and 12, 8 and 13, 7 and 11; the four centre points are paired thus: 4 and 2, 5 and 3; and the last card, No. 22, is taken separately. The significations are, of course, taken with regard to the relative positions of the cards, and their special reference to the central figure of the inquirer. This is a picturesque and simple way of consulting the cards, and will probably be a favorite with most people.

DIAGRAM OF THE GRAND STAR.

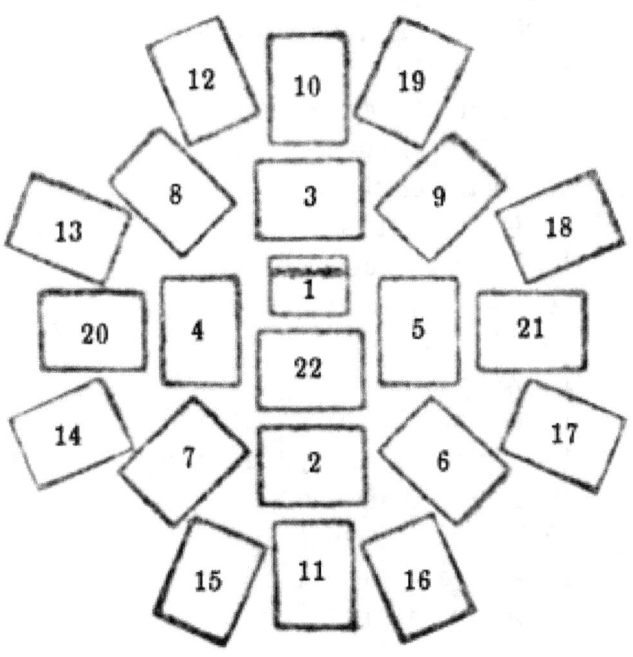

The central card, No. 1, represents the inquirer, and each card is numbered in the order in which it is taken from the pack.

We will take the king of hearts as representative of the inquirer, and the twenty-one cards come out in the following order:

1. King of hearts.
2. Ten of spades.
3. Ten of hearts.
4. Ace of hearts.
5. Nine of spades.
6. Ace of spades.
7. Nine of diamonds, reversed.
8. Queen of hearts.
9. Knave of diamonds.
10. Queen of spades.
11. Knave of clubs.
12. King of clubs.
13. Eight of clubs.
14. Queen of diamonds.
15. Nine of clubs, reversed.
16. King of spades.
17. Queen of clubs.
18. Eight of diamonds, reversed.
19. Ace of diamonds.
20. Knave of spades.
21. Knave of hearts.
22. Ace of clubs.

Before taking the above in pairs as directed, it will be well to glance at the groups contained in the star as it lies before us. We find:

Four aces. Love troubles and hasty news for the inquirer.
Three kings. Success in an important undertaking.
Four queens. A good deal of social intercourse.
Four knaves. Somewhat noisy conviviality.
Two tens. Unexpected good luck.
Three nines. Health, wealth, and happiness discounted by imprudence as one is reversed.

Two eights. Passing love fancies, one being reversed. The king of hearts, a fair, open-handed, good-natured man is the starting-point in reading the pairs which surround him. He is connected with (14) the queen of diamonds, a fair woman with a tendency to flirtation. She is amusing herself with (16) a very dark man, probably a lawyer, of an ambitious and not too scrupulous character, who does not wish well to the inquirer. The next pair (21) shows the knave of hearts, representing Cupid, or the thoughts of the one concerned, linked with (19) the ace of diamonds, a wedding ring. While this important item is occupying his thoughts he gives a small present (15), the nine of clubs, reversed, to (17) the queen of clubs, a charming dark lady, who is the real object of his affections. (20) The knave of spades, figuring a legal agent, or the wily lawyer's thoughts, makes mischief, and (18) the eight of diamonds, reversed, causes the inquirer's love-making to be unsuccessful. (6) The ace of spades warns the inquirer against false friends who will frustrate his matrimonial projects, and in (10) we find one of them, the queen of spades, a widow with possible designs upon him herself; (9) the knave of diamonds, reversed, shows the mischief-maker trying to breed strife with the inquirer's trusty friend (12), the king of clubs, and (8) the queen of hearts, a fair lovable woman possessing (13) eight of clubs, a dark person's affections; (7) the nine of diamonds, reversed, tells of a love quarrel, owing to (11) the knave of clubs, reversed, a harmless flirt The inquirer will get (4) the ace of hearts, a love letter, but his happiness will be succeeded by (2) the ten of spades, a card of bad import; (5) the nine of spades, tells of grief or sickness, possibly news of a death; but (3) the ten of hearts, counteracts the evil, and promises happiness to the inquirer, who shall triumph over the obstacles in his path, and find (22) joy in love and life.

IMPORTANT
QUESTIONS

*How to answer them - Specimen questions -
Cupid and Venus at work.*

HOW TO ANSWER
THEM.

WHEN an answer to an important question is
required, and the inquirer wishes to consult
the cards on the subject, the following simple
method may be adopted.

Let the question be asked by the inquirer, then
let the dealer take the pack of thirty-two
cards, which must be shuffled and cut in the
usual manner. The dealer throws out the first
eleven cards, which are useless, and proceeds
to turn up the others upon the table. The answer is determined by the absence or presence
of the special cards applying to each question
among the exposed twenty-one.

SPECIMEN QUESTIONS.

We will give some examples. Suppose the

question to be:—

"How far off is the wedding?"
The needful cards in this case are the queen of spades, who should come out with or near the queen of hearts, and the ace of spades, which should accompany the eight of diamonds. These must be taken in conjunction with the other eights - each of which signifies a year; the four nines - each of which stands for a month; and the four sevens - each of which represents a week. Supposing the above-named cards - the two queens, the ace of spades, and the eight of diamonds - should not come out in due order, or be absent altogether, it may be feared that the date is postponed to vanishing point.

"Have I real cause for jealousy?"
If the seven of diamonds comes out in the first fifteen cards, the answer is "Yes." If the five of hearts and the seven of clubs appear instead among the first fifteen, it means "No."

"Shall we be parted?" or *"Shall I sustain the loss of my goods?"*
If the four nines are included in the twenty-one cards, the answer is "Yes." Should the four kings and the four queens come out, the meaning is "No, never! "

"Shall I succeed in my present or projected undertaking?"

To ensure a favorable answer the four aces and the nine of hearts must come out. Should the nine of spades appear just before the card representing the inquirer, it prognosticates failure, sure and certain.

"Will the change of residence or condition that I am considering be satisfactory?"

Should this question be asked by the master or mistress of a house, or an employer of labor, a favorable answer is secured by the presence of the four knaves, the eight and ten of diamonds, and the ten of clubs. In the event of the inquirer being an employee, or a paid worker of any grade, the twenty-one cards must include the ten and seven of diamonds, the eight of spades, and the four queens, to ensure a satisfactory reply. In both cases the nine of diamonds means hindrances and delay in attaining success.

"What fortune does the future hold for this child?"

The four aces foretell good luck and a suitable marriage. If the child in question be a girl, the four eights and the king of hearts should come out to secure peace and concord for her ie the home of her husband.

CUPID AND VENUS AT WORK.

Among the many ways in which cards can be used to provide entertainment, seasoned with a spice of the unexplainable, the following round game may be given a prominent place.

The ace of diamonds is the most valuable asset in winning tricks, as it takes all the other cards. The pack of fifty-two cards is used.

The queen of hearts represents Venus.
The knave of hearts stands for Cupid.
The knave of diamonds, The knave of clubs, The knave of spades - all represent sweethearts.
The ace of hearts - a new house.
The ace of clubs - conquest.
The two of diamonds - the ring and marriage.
The twos of clubs, spades, and hearts - good luck.
The threes - show surprise.
The fours - that present conditions will remain unchanged.
The fives - lovers' meetings.
The sixes - pleasure.
The sevens - disappointment.
The eights - mirth.
The nines - changes.
The tens - marriage settlements.

The queens represent women.

The kings represent men.

Any number may take part in the game. The dealer Is chosen by lot, and when this has been settled, he or she proceeds to deal out the cards, leaving ten face downwards on the table. The stakes are agreed upon, and each player puts into the pool, the dealer being expected to pay double for the honor done to him by the fates.

The cards are then taken up, and each player looks at his own hand. The dealer calls for the queen of hearts, Venus, who ranks next to the ace of diamonds in value. Should any one have the ace of diamonds in his hand, he plays it straight out. Should the ace not be among those that have been dealt round, the queen of hearts is supreme, and the happy holder of Venus may look confidently forward to standing before the altar of Hymen during the current year. The ace of diamonds only counts as one card, but should any lucky player hold both Cupid and Venus in his hand he is entitled to clear the pool, and so end the game right off. In the event of the holder of these cards being married, their presence promises him some special stroke of good fortune. When the matrimonial cards are out, or proved absent, the game is played on similar lines to whist, the same order of precedence being observed in taking tricks, and the larger the number secured the better the luck of the winner during the current year. The nine of spades is the worst card in the pack, and the unfortunate holder has to pay for its presence in his hand by a treble stake to the pool. Should any player fail to win any tricks, he must pay in advance the stakes agreed upon for the next game.

MARRIAGE BY LOT.

For this appeal to the fates we require a pack of cards, a bag, and stakes either in money or counters. When the players have fixed upon their stakes and placed them in the pool, one of those playing must thoroughly shuffle the pack of cards and place them in the bag. The players then stand in a circle and draw three cards in turn from the bag as it is handed to each of them. Pairs of any kind win back the stakes paid by the holder, and promise good luck in the immediate future. The knave of hearts is proclaimed to represent Hymen. He wins double stakes, and is a happy augury that the holder will soon be united to the partner of his tit her choice. Should Venus, the queen of hearts, be found in the same hand, the owner takes the pool and wins the game. Fours and eights are losses and crosses, compelling a pre-arranged payment to the pool in addition to the usual stakes. A lady who draws three nines may resign herself to a life of single-blessedness, and the one who has three fives must prepare to cope with a bad husband.

YOUR FATE IN TWENTY CARDS.

Only three or four girls are required to pursue this search for hidden knowledge. All the kings, queens, knaves, aces, and threes must be taken from the pack and dealt round to the players. Each one examines her hand for an answer to her inward questionings. The one who holds the most kings possesses the largest number of friends. The one with most queens has a proportionate number of enemies. Where kings and queens are united, there is the promise of speedy and happy marriage. Should a queen come out with knaves, we may be sure that intrigues are being woven round some unlucky person. Knaves by themselves represent lovers. Threes are evil omens betokening great sorrow. A knave with four threes means that the fair holder will not enter the holy estate. A king with four threes encourages her to hope, for she has a good chance of matrimony. A queen with four threes is the worst combination a girl can draw, for it speaks of sorrow deepened by disgrace. Mixed hands have no special significance, nor is there any great meaning attached to the four aces. Where only two or three of one kind of card fall together, the meaning ascribed to the four collectively is lessened in proportion to the number held.

HEARTS ARE TRUMPS.

This game might by some be called an apology for whist. Four players, or three and a dummy, are necessary, and the whole pack is dealt out in the usual way. Hearts are trumps in every deal, and carry everything before them. The highest card is the queen, who is the goddess of love, and takes precedence of the ace, which only counts as one. The person on the left hand of the dealer leads trumps, and the stronger the hand the better the chances for love and marriage. The one who wins the largest number of tricks has, or will have, the most lovers. The presence of the king and queen of trumps in one hand is the sign of a speedy union of hearts, and of the approaching sound of wedding bells. A sorry fate awaits the luckless maid or youth who is without a heart—in the hand—for Cupid and Hymen have turned their faces away, and no luck will come of a love affair in that quarter. Where only one or two small trumps can be produced, the holder will have to wait long for wedded bliss. Each one plays quite independently of the others, and the one who undertakes dummy must not connect its cards in nay way with those he holds himself.

ANOTHER LOTTERY.

Put a well-shuffled pack of cards into a bag deep enough to prevent the contents from being seen. An uneven number of girls must then form a ring round the one holding the bag, and each must draw a card. The cards thus drawn must then all be exposed, as they have to be compared. The lucky lady who draws the highest card will be the first to be led to the altar. She who draws the lowest will have to emulate Mariana of the Moated Grange, and resign herself to the fact that "he cometh not" for many weary days to follow. Any one drawing the ace of spades may cheerfully prepare for the pleasures of a bachelor life. The nine of hearts is the presage of serious trouble, coming to the holder through loving "not wisely but too well."

ITALIAN METHOD.

ONLY thirty-two cards are used for the Italian method of fortune-telling, all the numbers under seven, except the ace, being taken out of each suit. This reduced pack - containing the ace, king, queen, knave, ten, nine, eight, and seven of the four suits - must be carefully shuffled and cut, with the left hand of course, by the inquirer. The one who is going to act as interpreter then takes the pack, and turns them up three at a time. Should three cards of one suit be turned up at once, they are all laid upon the table, face upwards; if only two of a suit come out together, the higher card is selected; if all three belong to different suits, they are all rejected.

When the pack has been dealt out in this manner the cards that have not been chosen are taken up, shuffled, and cut a second time. The deal by threes is then repeated until there are fifteen cards upon the table. They must be placed in line, from left to right, as they appear.

It is absolutely necessary that the card representing the inquirer should be among those on the table. Some authorities maintain, however, that in the event of its not coming out during the deals, the whole process must be repeated until it makes its appearance. Others again take the card out, and place it on the table when fourteen others have been selected. The next step is to count five cards from the representative one and to continue counting in fifths from each fifth card until all have been included, or the counting has come back to the representative. The signification of every card is read as it is reached, due notice being taken as to whether it is reversed or not, and the surrounding circumstances must also be balanced by the interpreter.

When this reading is complete the fifteen cards must be paired, one from each end of the line being taken and read together, while the remaining odd one must be dealt with separately.

The third process is to shuffle and cut the fifteen cards, and deal them out into five small packs: one for the lady herself; one for the house; one for those who do not expect it; one for those who do expect it; one for the surprise; and one, which is not to be covered, for consolation. When the fifteen cards have been dealt out, it will be seen that four of the packs contain three cards, and the fifth only two. These must all be turned face upwards and read in separate packs, but with the connecting idea that they all refer to the fortune of the inquirer.

AN EXAMPLE.

Let us imagine that a very fair lady, represented by the queen of diamonds, is seeking to read her fortune. The fifteen cards come out in the following order:

The queen of diamonds; nine of diamonds, reversed; queen of hearts; king of spades; ten of diamonds; seven of diamonds, reversed; knave of hearts, reversed; ten of hearts; knave of diamonds; ace of diamonds, reversed; knave of spades; nine of spades; king of clubs; ten of spades, reversed; ace of hearts.

We begin to count from the queen of diamonds, the representative card, and find the nine of diamonds to be the fifth from it. By this first count we see from the nine being reversed that there is a love quarrel troubling the inquirer. Starting again from the nine we come to the queen of hearts, a mild, good-natured, but not very wise woman, who is probably the tool of the next fifth card, the king of spades, a crafty, ambitious man, and an enemy to the queen of diamonds. Our next count is to the ten of diamonds, which speaks of a journey for the inquirer. Passing on to the seven of diamonds, reversed, we get hold of a foolish scandal connected with, if not entirely caused by, the next count, which is the knave of hearts, reversed, and stands for a military man who is very discontented with the treatment he has received at the hands of the fair inquirer. She will, however, triumph over this foolish annoyance, for the ten of hearts comes next in order, and counteracts the harm involved by the other cards.

Our gentle lady has, unfortunately, an unfaithful friend in the knave of diamonds; and he is
followed by the ace of diamonds, reversed,
which portends a letter on the way containing
bad news. The writer of this is a dark young
man of no social position, and he probably is
the servant of one who is dear to the queen of
diamonds. The bad news is found in the next
count, the nine of spades, which tells of sickness affecting the king of clubs, the warm-
hearted, chivalrous man who occupies the first
place in the inquirer's affections. The last
count but one brings us to the ten of spades,
reversed, by which we know that the lady's
sorrow will be but brief; and it is followed by
the ace of hearts, a love letter containing the
good news of her lover's recovery.

NOTICE THE GROUPS.

Before proceeding to pair the cards, we may
as well note the groups as they have come out
in the fifteen. The six diamonds point to there
being plenty of money; the two tens tell of a
change of residence, either brought about by
marriage, or by the journey read in the ten of
diamonds; the presence of three knaves betokens false friends, though as one is reversed,
their power of doing harm is lessened; two
queens indicate gossip and the revealing of

secrets; the two aces imply an attempted plot, but it is frustrated by the one being reversed; the two nines also point to riches.

HOW THE PAIRS WORK OUT.

The two end cards of the fifteen are taken up together, so that the pairs shall work out thus: The queen of diamonds and the nine of spades, implying that sickness and trouble will affect the inquirer; the ten of diamonds pairs with the ten of hearts, and they signify a wedding; the knaves of diamonds and spades coming together show evil intentions towards the inquirer; the king of clubs and the ace of hearts tell of the lover and the love letter; the inverted nine of diamonds pairing with the knave of spades, tells of a love quarrel, in which a dark young man, wanting in refinement, is concerned; the reversed seven of diamonds pairs with the knave of hearts, also inverted, and tells of a foolish scandal instigated by the ungallant soldier who is suffering from wounded vanity; the inverted ace of diamonds comes out with the queen of hearts, telling of a letter containing unpleasant news from a fair, good-natured woman; while the remaining card, the ten of spades, being inverted, speaks of brief sorrow for the inquirer.

THE FIVE PACKS.

Our next step is to deal out the five packs as already directed. The first one - for the lady herself - contains three cards, two of which are bad, but their harm is largely discounted by the ten of hearts. In the nine of spades we read of the trouble caused by her lover's illness; the ten of spades betokens the tears she will shed while the beloved life is in danger; the ten of hearts speaks of happiness triumphing over sorrow.

The second pack - for the house - contains a flush of diamonds, the ten, the ace, and the knave. There is plenty of money in the house: the ten speaks of a journey, possibly resulting in a change of residence; the ace, being reversed, tells of a letter on the way containing unpleasant news (probably connected with the removal), from the knave, who is a faithless friend, and is to blame for the annoyance. The third pack - for those who do not expect - consists of three court cards, which taken together foretell gaiety of some sort. We find the inquirer, personated by the queen of diamonds, in the society of the knaves of spades and hearts, the latter reversed, and consequently we know that she will be troubled by some unfriendly schemes, in which the dark, undesirable young man and the disappointed officer will be concerned. The inversion of the one knave counteracts the intended harm.

The fourth pack - for *those who do expect* - contains the queen of hearts, the king of spades, and the seven of diamonds, inverted. These indicate that the fair woman of gentle and affectionate nature will be exposed to scandal, seven of diamonds reversed; through the agency of the king of spades, an ambitious untrustworthy lawyer who is her enemy.

The fifth pack, consisting of only two cards (the ace of hearts and the nine of diamonds), is for the surprise, and we learn that a love letter, the ace, will be delayed, the nine; but the consolation card is the king of clubs, the dark, warm-hearted man, who will come in person to his lady-love.

The above example has been taken in the plainest, most straightforward manner with just the most apparent reading of the cards given as an illustration of the method. Those who spend time and thought on the subject will soon get to see more of the "true inwardness" of the cards with respect to their relative positions, and their influence one upon another. Various experiments with this plan of fortune-telling will give rise to curious combinations, and perhaps startling developments, as the one acting for the inquirer gains in knowledge and confidence.

Finis.

OTHER TITLES

Our list of available titles grows monthly. Please check the website for the most up to date listings: www.creolemoon.com.

Title	Price
Crossroads Mamas 105 Spiritual Baths For Every Occasion By Denise Alvarado and Madrina Angelique	$9.95
Workin' in da Boneyard By Denise Alvarado and Madrina Angelique	$9.95
Day of the Dead Handbook By Denise Alvarado	$13.00
The Hoodoo Almanac 2012 By Denise Alvarado, Carolina Dean and Alyne Pustanio	$19.95
The Hoodoo Almanac 2013 By Denise Alvarado, Carolina Dean and Alyne Pustanio	$19.95
Voodoo Dolls in Magick and Ritual By Denise Alvarado	$19.95
A Guide to Serving the Seven African Powers By Denise Alvarado	$19.95
Purloined Stories and Early Tales of Old New Orleans By Alyne Pustanio	$15.95
Gypsy Wisdom, Spells Charms and Folklore By Denise Alvarado	$13.00
Fortune Telling with Playing Cards By P.R.S. Foli	$9.00
Hoodoo and Conjure Quarterly #2 By Denise Alvarado	$19.95
The True Grimoire By King Solomon	$6.95

Creole Moon Publications Order Form

Item #	Description	Qty.	Price	Subtotal

Order Total _____

Tax _____

Shipping _____

Total _____

_____

Name

_____

Address

_____

Phone

Shipping is $6.00 for the first title and $3.00 for each additional title. Domestic shipping through mail order only. International customers, please order through the website: www.creolemoon.com.

Please make your check or money order out to Denise Alvarado.

Send check or money order to:

Denise Alvarado
P.O. Box 25687
Prescott Valley, AZ 86312